1.7/0.5

How Many Days?

by Katherine Krieg

Say Hello to Amicus Readers.

You'll find our helpful dog, Amicus, chasing a ball—to let you know the reading level of a book.

1

Learn to Read

Frequent repetition, high frequency words, and close photo-text matches introduce familiar topics and provide ample support for brand new readers.

2

Read Independently

Some repetition is mixed with varied sentence structures and a select amount of new vocabulary words are introduced with text and photo support.

3

Read to Know More

Interesting facts and engaging art and photos give fluent readers fun books both for reading practice and to learn about new topics.

Amicus Readers are published by Amicus
P.O. Box 1329, Mankato, MN 56002
www.amicuspublishing.us

Photo Credits: iStockphoto, cover, 5, 8; Shutterstock Images, 1; Songquan Deng/Shutterstock Images, 3, 14–15; Fuse/Thinkstock, 6–7; iStock/Thinkstock, 11, 16 (top); Smolych Iryna/Shutterstock Images, 12–13; Sean Locke Photography/Shutterstock Images, 16 (bottom)

Produced for Amicus by The Peterson Publishing Company and Red Line Editorial.

Editor Jenna Gleisner
Designer Becky Daum

Library of Congress
Cataloging-in-Publication Data
Krieg, Katherine, author.
  How many days? / by Katherine Krieg.
    pages cm. -- (Amicus readers level 2) (Measuring time)
  Summary: 'Introduces activities young readers experience in a matter of days, such as eating three meals or touring a city, while teaching ways to measure a day and how it compares to hours and weeks.'-- Provided by publisher.
  Audience: K to grade 3.
  ISBN 978-1-60753-723-6 (library binding)
  ISBN 978-1-60753-827-1 (ebook)
  1. Time--Juvenile literature. 2. Time measurements--Juvenile literature. I. Title.
  QB209.5.K744 2014
  529.7--dc23
                                2014049950

Printed in Malaysia
10 9 8 7 6 5 4 3 2 1

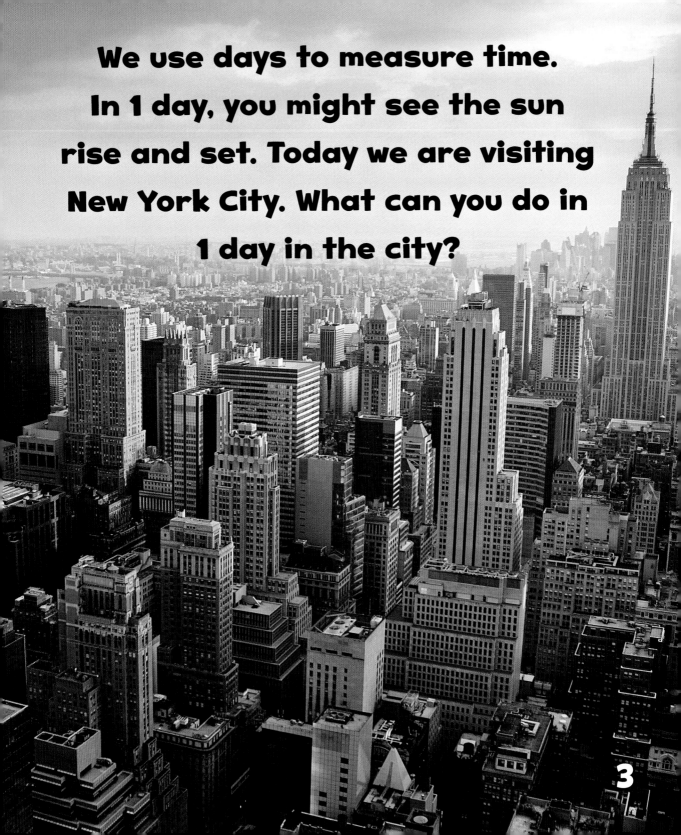

We use days to measure time. In 1 day, you might see the sun rise and set. Today we are visiting New York City. What can you do in 1 day in the city?

3

Payton eats 3 meals in **1 day.** She has breakfast, lunch, and dinner. There are lots of fun places to eat in the city.

Morning, afternoon, and evening are all parts of **1 day.**

Evan and his mom tour the city. The tour lasts all afternoon.

7

Blake's family stays overnight in a hotel. They are in the city for

24 hours.

That is the same as

1 day.

Anna's family visits the city for **3 days.** Her mom shows her the days on a calendar. Each day is 1 square on the calendar.

June

SUNDAY	MONDAY	TUESDAY	WEDNESDAY	THURSDAY	FRIDAY	SATURDAY
	1	2	3	4	5	6
7	8	9	10	11	12	13
14	15	16	17	18	19	20
21	22	23	24	25	26	27
28	29	30				

1 day

Jenny and her dad go to the zoo and see a play in the city. They stay for

7 days.

That is

1 week!

There are many places to
see in just 1 day.
How many days would
you like to spend in
the city?

15

Measuring Days

APRIL
15

1 day

1 day

JANUARY

SUNDAY	MONDAY	TUESDAY	WEDNESDAY	THURSDAY	FRIDAY	SATURDAY
				1	2	3
4	5	6	7	8	9	10
11	12	13	14	15	16	17
18	19	20	21	22	23	24
25	26	27	28	29	30	31

1 month

1 week

16